# Long Ago AND Far Away

# Ancient Egypt

Amy Tiehel

PURPLE TOAD
PUBLISHING

Printing
1     __     2     3     4     5     6     7     8     9

Ancient China
Ancient Egypt
Ancient Rome
The Aztecs
Mesopotamia

**Publisher's Cataloging-in-Publication Data**
Tiehel, Amy.
  Ancient Egypt / Amy Tiehel.
    p. cm.
Includes bibliographic references and index.
ISBN 9781624691263
1. Egypt—Civilization—Juvenile literature. 2. Egypt—Antiquities—Juvenile literature. I. Series: Long ago and far away.
 DT43 2015
 932.01

                        Library of Congress Control Number:  2014945178

**eBook ISBN**: 9781624691270

**ABOUT THE AUTHOR**
Amy Tiehel produced and wrote scripts for the children's educational video series *Black Americans of Achievement, Earth at Risk* and *Multi-cultural Peoples of North America* for Fabian-Baber/Schlessinger Video Productions. She won her eighth-grade science award for a report on ancient Egypt, igniting her desire to be an Egyptologist. Amy lives in Philadelphia, Pennsylvania, with her family and cat, Queen Sheba.

**PUBLISHER'S NOTE**

# Contents

# 1

# A Land of Sand and Soil

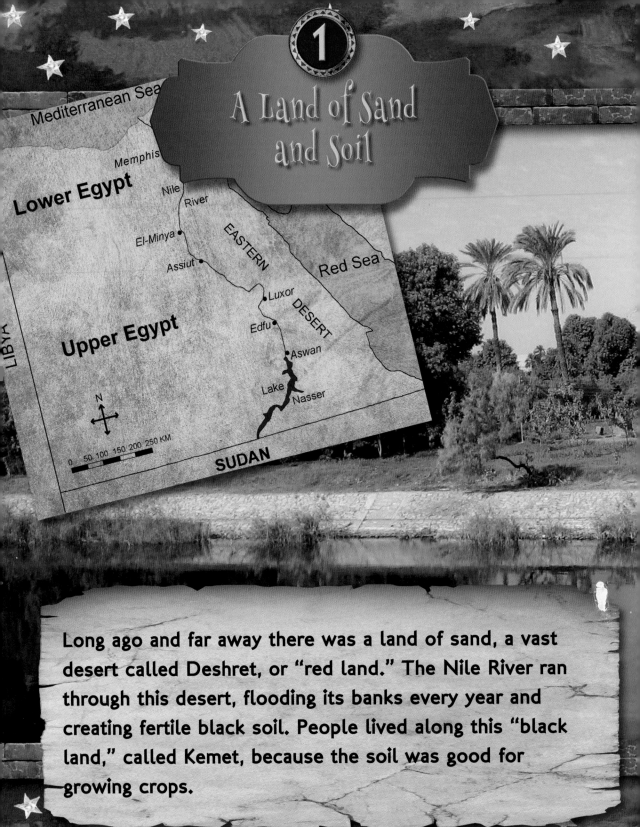

Mediterranean Sea

Lower Egypt

Memphis

Nile
River

El-Minya

Assiut

EASTERN

Red Sea

Luxor

DESERT

Edfu

Upper Egypt

Aswan

Lake
Nasser

LIBYA

N

0  50 100 150 200 250 KM

SUDAN

Long ago and far away there was a land of sand, a vast desert called Deshret, or "red land." The Nile River ran through this desert, flooding its banks every year and creating fertile black soil. People lived along this "black land," called Kemet, because the soil was good for growing crops.

The Nile River

The country was also divided into Upper and Lower parts. About 5,000 years ago, a pharaoh, or king, united the two halves, creating what we know as ancient Egypt.

Cleopatra

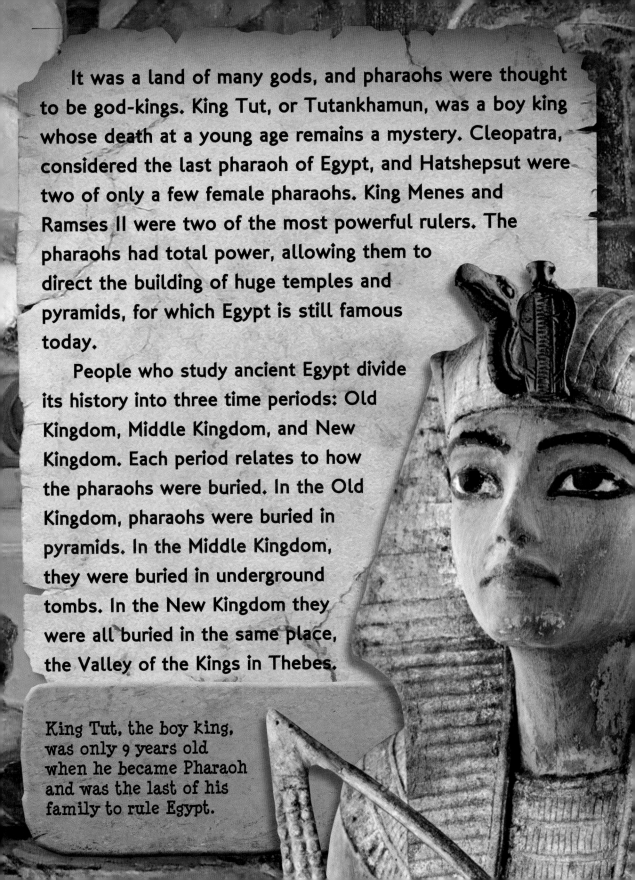

It was a land of many gods, and pharaohs were thought to be god-kings. King Tut, or Tutankhamun, was a boy king whose death at a young age remains a mystery. Cleopatra, considered the last pharaoh of Egypt, and Hatshepsut were two of only a few female pharaohs. King Menes and Ramses II were two of the most powerful rulers. The pharaohs had total power, allowing them to direct the building of huge temples and pyramids, for which Egypt is still famous today.

People who study ancient Egypt divide its history into three time periods: Old Kingdom, Middle Kingdom, and New Kingdom. Each period relates to how the pharaohs were buried. In the Old Kingdom, pharaohs were buried in pyramids. In the Middle Kingdom, they were buried in underground tombs. In the New Kingdom they were all buried in the same place, the Valley of the Kings in Thebes.

King Tut, the boy king, was only 9 years old when he became Pharaoh and was the last of his family to rule Egypt.

Under the leadership of the pharaohs, Egyptian culture flourished. Egyptians developed a written language using symbols called hieroglyphs. They also wrote poems, stories, and detailed factual records. Artists and craftsmen created paintings, sculptures, and tomb monuments. They forged delicate jewelry, pots, and glassworks.

Egypt was a land of abundance, and the people believed their land was sacred. The Nile provided fish, ducks, and geese. The Egyptians raised oxen, goats, sheep, and pigs. They grew wheat and barley and also flax, which they used to make linen cloth. The land was rich in copper, which the Egyptians used to make tools, and bronze and gold, which were turned into jewelry.

Hieroglyphs - The origin of the word hieroglyph is Greek; hiero means holy and glyph means writing, thus holy writing.

Flax - The flax plant was grown along the banks of the Nile River and could be harvested by pulling it out by the roots.

Egyptian amulets were usually animal shaped. People carried or wore them because they believed they had protective powers.

Pharaoh Amos rides into battle in a horse drawn chariot, which was brought to Egypt by the Hyksos.

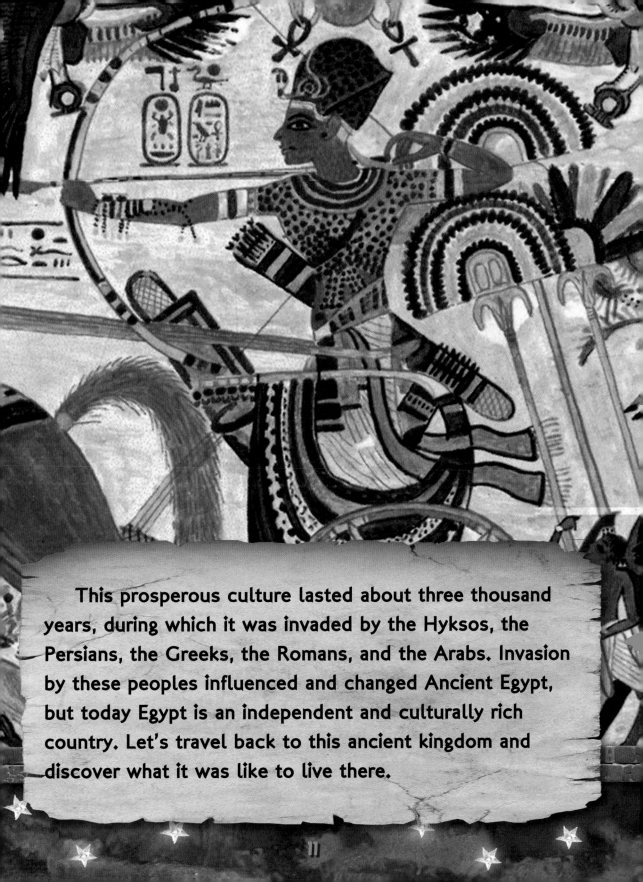

This prosperous culture lasted about three thousand years, during which it was invaded by the Hyksos, the Persians, the Greeks, the Romans, and the Arabs. Invasion by these peoples influenced and changed Ancient Egypt, but today Egypt is an independent and culturally rich country. Let's travel back to this ancient kingdom and discover what it was like to live there.

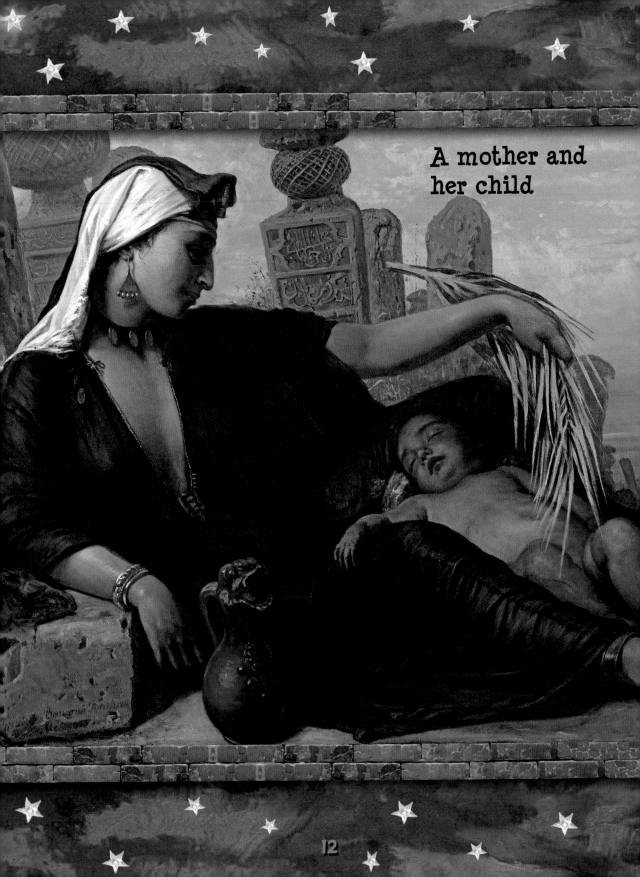

A mother and
her child

# 2

# Family Life

If you were a child in ancient Egypt, you would probably have many brothers and sisters, as the Egyptians had large families. They believed family included their deceased relatives, and they had statues of their ancestors on display in the home.

   Boys were responsible for taking care of their aging parents and would become the head of the household at a young age. At fourteen they stopped wearing the sidelock hairstyle, a ponytail on the side of their shaved head, to show they were now a grownup.

A typical boy's hairstyle

Girls helped raise their younger siblings. They learned household chores from their mother, such as baking bread and weaving. They stayed at home until about the age of fourteen, when they were married, at which time they went to live in their husband's home. Egyptians did not have wedding ceremonies. Instead they would have a lively procession from the bride's home to the groom's home, and then they would have a feast.

Egyptians lived in mud-brick huts with small windows, which kept the heat out. The family often slept on the roof where they could feel cool breezes. A courtyard outside was used for cooking. It also housed cattle and pets: dogs, cats, monkeys, and birds.

Mud brick houses - Houses had bricks made of straw and mud. Doors were built a few feet off the ground to keep the sand from coming in.

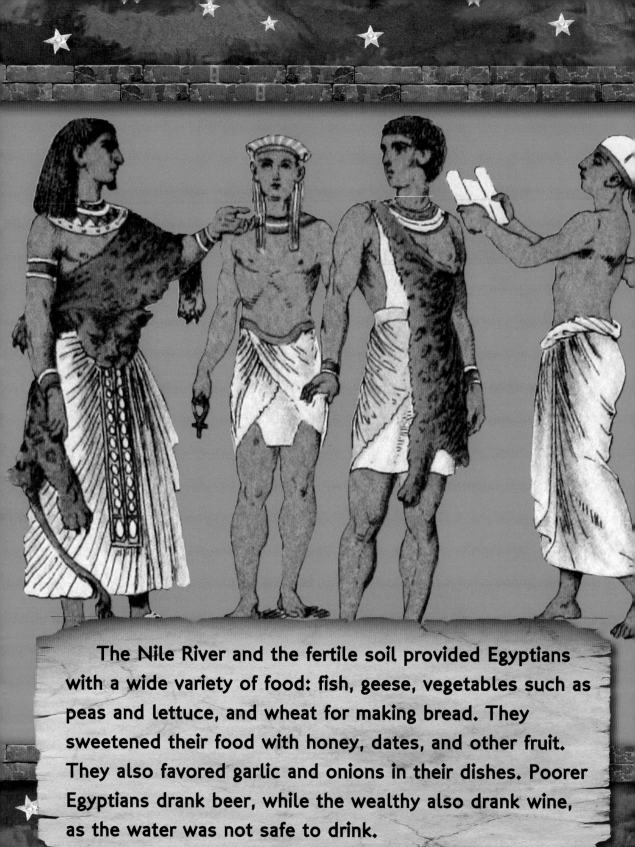

The Nile River and the fertile soil provided Egyptians with a wide variety of food: fish, geese, vegetables such as peas and lettuce, and wheat for making bread. They sweetened their food with honey, dates, and other fruit. They also favored garlic and onions in their dishes. Poorer Egyptians drank beer, while the wealthy also drank wine, as the water was not safe to drink.

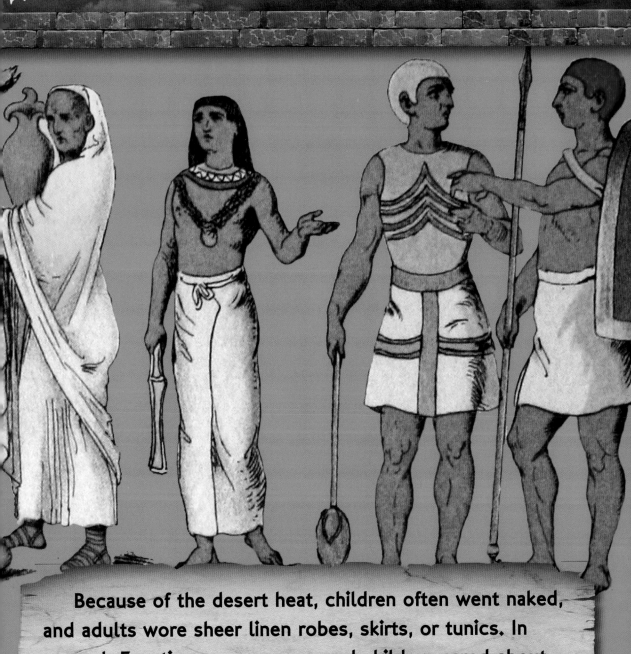

Because of the desert heat, children often went naked, and adults wore sheer linen robes, skirts, or tunics. In general, Egyptian men, women, and children cared about their appearance and wore colorful jewelry and makeup. They circled their eyes with kohl, or black eyeliner, to protect their eyes from infection and from the glare of the sun.

# School and Work

# 3

Children in ancient Egypt began work at a young age, helping at home and carrying food to field workers. They also joined in the harvest, scaring away birds and gathering grain. However, wealthy families had servants or slaves to do their work, so their children didn't have to help.

The Egyptian tradition was that boys learned their father's trade, such as carpentry or metalworking. Families who could afford school sent their boys to study arithmetic, reading, writing, and religion.

A scribe was a person who wrote books and other written works by hand. Scribes were trained in places called Houses of Life, where they learned to do hieroglyphics, a form of writing that used pictures for words.

It took as many as ten years to learn, so scribes were greatly respected in Ancient Egypt.

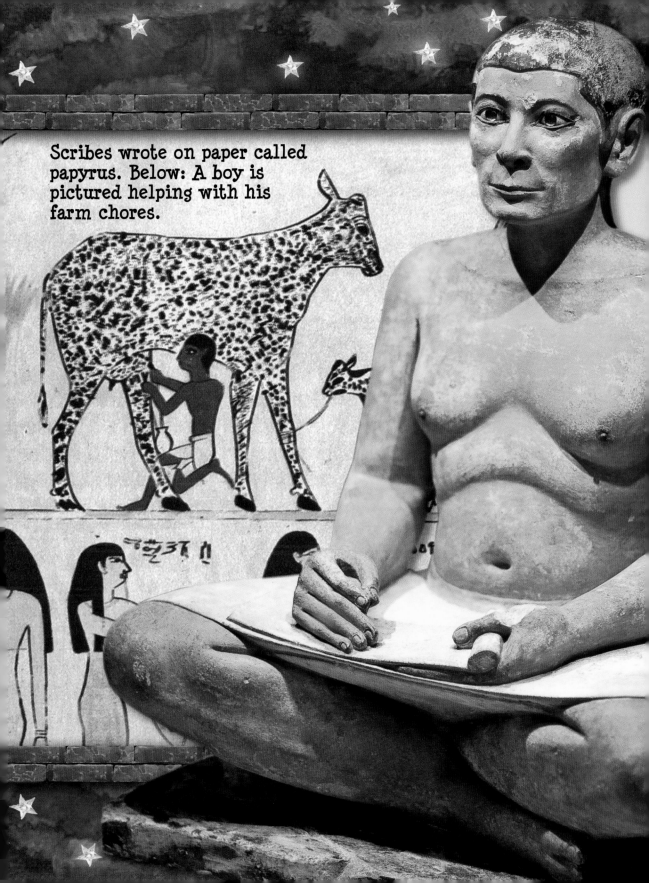

Scribes wrote on paper called papyrus. Below: A boy is pictured helping with his farm chores.

Some girls were taught how to read and write at home. A few even became doctors.

In ancient Egyptian society, most people were farmers and peasants—people who grew food and worked for the royal family. Some were skilled craftspeople: carpenters, masons, jewelers, stonecutters, or painters.

Egyptian wives and mothers were highly respected in this ancient society. Women did most of the weaving and the household work, but they also helped in the fields. Women could also find work in the royal court as entertainers or as maids and nannies.

Watching over all was the vizier, or chief minister, who represented the pharaoh in the law courts. The pharaoh and his family were at the top of this society, in charge of everyone.

An ancient model of women working in a kitchen, baking. To make bread, women first ground the grain then mixed and kneaded all of the ingredients together by hand.

# 4

# Play Time

Despite working hard from a young age, Egyptian children still found time for play. Babies were given rattles of dried wood or gourds with bells or pebbles in them. They also played with cloth dolls and clay animals.

When playing outside, children raced each other and rode piggyback, trying to knock each other off. Boys arm-wrestled and played tug-of-war and leapfrog. They also used balls made out of clay or cloth for many different games.

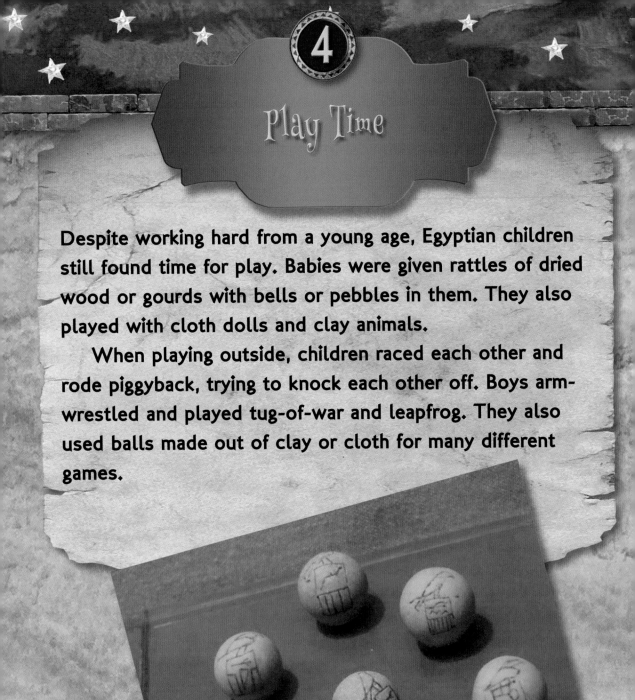

Marbles, a linen ball, and a top, all from Ancient Egypt.

Girls juggled and played a game of throwing and catching a ball while clapping in between. They also played a game called pressing the grapes, which consisted of dancing in a circle while holding hands.

Most children and adults enjoyed the board games hounds and jackals, from the Middle Kingdom, and senet, from the Old Kingdom. Senet, which means "passing," was played on a board with thirty spaces. Each player moved around the board, avoiding hazards. The player to get all of his or her pieces off the board first won the game.

Senet—The pieces in Senet were usually cones and reels and the dice were four painted sticks or knucklebones.

# Gods and the Afterlife

# 5

Egyptians believed in many gods and had festivals to honor them. The Festival of Opet was celebrated yearly when the Nile River flooded. A statue of the sun god Amun-Re was carried in a procession for all to see. People made bouquets from flowers and enjoyed singing, music, and worship. The festival lasted for several weeks.

The Egyptians worshipped hundreds of gods, but the source of all life was the god Atum. Atum was thought to be the creator of all other gods. Geb was the earth god and Nut was the sky goddess. Osiris, Isis, Seth, and Horus were also major gods.

The afterlife, or life after death, had great meaning for the Egyptians, so it was important to be buried properly. They thought that the soul, Ba, lived on and that death was the beginning of a great journey. Preparations for death were sacred. Egyptians were buried with everything they needed to survive the afterlife. This included their body, so it was preserved as a mummy.

Isis and Osiris. Isis was the goddess of healing and motherly love.  Osiris was the god of the underworld.

To mummify a body, an embalmer took out the liver and other organs and placed them in special jars, called canopic jars. Then the body was packed with natron, a chemical that dried and preserved the flesh. The body was blessed and then wrapped in linen bandages and covered with a mask.

The mummy of an everyday Egyptian could be buried in the desert or in a simple grave. Pharaohs were buried in grand tombs or pyramids with all of their possessions: furniture, food, mummified animals, chariots, statues, jewels, weaponry, and sometimes entire ships.

On the walls of the burial chambers were colorful paintings of daily life and maps to the underworld. Many of these tombs and pyramids still survive. The largest is the Great Pyramid of Giza.

Can you imagine what it must have been like to be a boy or girl in Egypt, thousands of years ago? The ancient Egyptians believed in life after death—and the paintings, treasures, hieroglyphics, and pyramids they left behind allow them to live on.

The Pyramids of Gaza and an enclosed mummy.

## Books

Cobblestone Editors. *If I Were a Kid in Ancient Egypt: Children of the Ancient World.* Peterborough, NH: Cricket Books, 2007.

Hart, George. *DK Eyewitness Books: Ancient Egypt.* New York: DK Children's Books, 2008.

Van Vleet, Carmela. *Great Ancient Egypt Projects: You Can Build Yourself.* White River Junction, VT: Nomad Press, 2006.

Williams, Marcia. *Ancient Egypt: Tales of Gods and Pharaohs.* Somerville, MA: Candlewick Press, 2013.

## Works Consulted

Hart, Dr. George (editor). *Ancient Egypt (The Nature Company Discoveries Library).* Time Life Books, 1995.

The Metropolitan Museum of Art: Game of Hounds and Jackals.
http://www.metmuseum.org/collection/the-collection-online/search/543867

Millmore, Mark. *Imagining Egypt, A Living Portrait of the Time of the Pharaohs.* New York: Black Dog & Leventhal Publishers, Inc., 2007.

Morelle, Rebecca. "New Timeline for Origin of Ancient Egypt." *BBC News,* September 3, 2013. http://www.bbc.com/news/science-environment-23947820

*Per-ankh:* The House of Life
http://www.reshafim.org.il/ad/egypt/institutions/house_of_life.htm

Shaw, Ian (editor). *The Oxford History of Ancient Egypt.* Oxford: Oxford University Press, 2000.

Tames, Richard. *Ancient Egyptian Children (People in the Past.)* Chicago: Reed Educational and Professional Publishing, 2003.

Tour Egypt: The Opet Festival
http://www.touregypt.net/featurestories/opetfestival1.htm

The Walters Art Gallery: Senet
http://art.thewalters.org/detail/39889/senet-game-piece-2/

## On the Internet

Donn, Lin. *Ancient Egypt for Kids.*
http://egypt.mrdonn.org/index.html

*Experience Ancient Egypt*
http://www.experience-ancient-egypt.com/

Sites In Teaching: *Discovering Ancient Egypt*
http://www.discoveringegypt.com/

## Games

Ancient Egyptian Game of Senet
http://shop.discoveringegypt.com/ancient-egyptian-game-of-senet/

Hieroglyphic Typewriter
http://www.discoveringegypt.com/hieroglyphic-typewriter.html

# Glossary

**Amun-Re** (AH-muhn-RAY)—King of the Egyptian gods.

**Ancestor** (AN-ses-ter)—A person from whom one is descended.

**Arabs** (AIR-ubs)—People from the Arabian Peninsula living in the Middle East and North Africa.

**Atum** (AH-tum)—An ancient Egyptian creator god.

**Ba** (BAH)—The ancient Egyptian word for "soul."

**Bronze** (BRONZ)—A metal made mostly of copper and tin.

**Canopic** (kuh-NOH-pik) jar—A jar used to store human organs as part of the mummification process.

**Cleopatra** (klee-oh-PAT-ruh)—Queen of Egypt from 51-49 and 48-30 BCE.

**Deshret** (desh-RET)—"Red land," the Egyptian desert on either side of the Nile River.

**Embalm** (em-BALM)—To treat a dead body with chemicals to preserve it.

**Fertile** (FUR-tul)—Capable of producing crops abundantly.

**Flax**—A plant that is grown for its fiber and seeds.

**Geb**—God of the earth, and father of Isis and Osiris.

**Giza** (GEE-za)—A city in Egypt near the Nile River.

**Hatshepsut** (hat-SHEP-soot)—Queen of Egypt from 1473 to 1458 BCE.

**Hieroglyph** (HY-roh-glif)—Symbols that stand for words or sounds.

**Hyksos** (HIK-sohs)—Nomadic people who conquered Egypt, thought to have migrated from Asia.

**Kemet** (kuh-MET)—"Black land," the name for ancient Egypt.

**Kohl**—A black powder used for eye makeup.

**Linen** (LIN-un)—Light cloth made from flax.

**Mason** (MAY-sun)—A person who builds with bricks, stone, tiles or blocks.

**Menes** (MEE-neez)—The unifier of Egypt and first king, who ruled around 3000 BCE.

**Mummification** (muh-mih-fi-KAY-shun)—The process of preserving a dead body as a mummy.

**Natron** (NAY-tron)—A mineral salt used in embalming dead bodies.

**Nut** (NOOT)—Goddess of the sky.

**Pharaoh** (FAH-roh)—An ancient Egyptian King.

**Papyrus** (pa-PIE-rus)—A thin paper like material made from the papyrus plant.

**Persians** (PER-shuns)—People from the country of Iran.

**Ramses** II (RAM-uh-seez)—King of Egypt from 1279 to 1213 BCE.

**Scribe**—A person who is trained to write or copy words.

**Senet** (SEH-net)—"Game of passing," an Egyptian board game.

**Sidelock** (SYD-lok)—A hairstyle marked by a ponytail on the side of a shaved head.

**Tunic** (TOO-nik)—A loose-fitting outer garment.

**Tutankhamun** (too-tahng-KAH-mun)—Boy king of Egypt who ruled from c.1336 to 1327 BCE.

**Vizier** (vih-ZEER)—A high-ranking official.

# Index